TESTED FOREX STRATEGIES

Learn The Proven Strategies Of Forex Trading

WAYNE WALKER

Contents

Disclaimer

The advice and strategies contained in this book are based on my personal trading experience and opinions, and may not be appropriate for your trading situation.

INTRODUCTION

nstead of spending thousands of dollars, or reading 300 page books, you can learn the realistic essentials of trading in dramatically less time. This is not "watered down" with short cuts. The guide contains the techniques that professional and successful traders use. These concepts have been tested and backed by client testimonials from my seminars.

My firm awards a trading diploma based on these techniques that has been adopted by several universities.

WHAT IS FOREX?

n this chapter we will examine the foreign exchange market, the participants, what makes the market move, and why you should want to trade it.

So what is Forex (Foreign Exchange) or FX as many people call it? , it is the world's most liquid market. The average daily turnover is over 4 trillion US Dollars. This is a huge number, but to put it in perspective, one day of FX is roughly 2 to 3 months of trading volume on the New York Stock Exchange. This is powerful, it means a lot of liquidity and that a lot of people are involved in it.

It is OTC traded, meaning over the counter with no central exchange, in contrast to the equity or commodity markets where there are central exchanges that buyers and sellers meet. With FX, it is just you and your broker/dealer.

It is open for 24/5 trading, from Sydney 5 AM on Mondays to New York 5 PM on Fridays. Plenty of time, allowing for round the clock trading.

Centers and Participants

Who are the people that are involved in this FX phenomenon?

First we will take a look at the FX centers. The main centers of FX are the UK, US, and Japan. They are responsible for the bulk of the trading Australia, Singapore and Switzerland are also important players in the market, but the main players remain US, UK and Japan.

Banks and Financial Institutions

It is primarily major banks and financial institutions, they account for roughly 50% of the transactions. They trade electronically amongst themselves.

The central banks are also involved and their role is to intervene in an attempt to influence the value of their currencies.

Let us take a closer look at this. Maybe the most famous of central banks, the Federal Reserve Board, they and also the Bank of Japan, are at times known to be active participants in the market in an attempt to influence the strength or weakness of their currencies. A FX trader must be aware of the roles that they play.

Additional Participants

There are now FX hedge funds, years ago if you mentioned FX hedge funds most people would not know what you were talking about, because they did not exist. There are funds that trade either one particular currency or regional currencies, and for those that have an interest they are available.

Other participants are the brokers, both voice and electronic, they serve as intermediaries between banks and dealers. Banks and dealers turn to them for assistance in finding the best deals, but the days of voice brokers are numbered, because most activity now is electronic. There are many firms today that have dealer free desks.

Corporations are also involved, especially the multinationals who have currency risk that needs to be hedged and also for their own speculation. Several international corporations have their own trading desks which they use for prop or proprietary trading.

A hedging example could be, an American company purchases goods from Japan and they receive an invoice that will be due in Yens. To hedge against a potential loss, where the amount due might increase in USD due to fluctuations in the currency, they open a position in the market.

A note on hedging, what we are discussing is removing the risk of holding a particular asset. The main focus is not necessarily on making a profit. For example, in the futures market we might have a wheat farmer and he is what we would say, long wheat. He is afraid of a price fall, so he sells wheat futures contracts to be hedged in case of a fall. If prices do fall, he would make up the loss on the down side. He does not make a profit, but he does remove the risk of holding the wheat.

Private Purposes

For most of us, international travel is a common activity, therefore most people when travelling will need the currency of their destination.

Our overseas purchases are also a factor. If you are sitting in New York and are looking to buy a pair of shoes in London over the internet, normally they will not accept USD, so you will need to convert to British Pounds.

There is also speculation, and this has been one of the main drivers in turning FX into a very hot market over the past few years where people are buying and selling just for speculative purposes.

What moves FX?

What is going on in the market? Why does it move? Several things, it could be rumors , it could be from government intervention, for example if the Bank of Japan enters the market in an attempt to shore up the Yen to prevent a slide, some traders might take it as a cue to start being long (buying) Yens and short (selling) the other crosses against it.

Data

Non-farm payroll is one of the major reports. Also whenever there is a rate decision from the Fed, Bank of England, ECB, or Bank of Japan etc., these are known market movers.

Wars, terrorist acts, whether it is events in the Middle East or other hot spots in the world, they can and do affect the market and in some cases quite drastically.

Central banks, as we touched on with their intervention, sometimes will do as we say "talk down" a currency. For example, bank governors without entering the market with direct intervention can influence it. It could be something where a central bank governor passes a remark at a news conference saying "I think the currency is getting overvalued and we might need to do something about it" or in some cases they might say "the strength of the currency is of concern to us and it's affecting our competitiveness". Depending on who is saying it, the results can be dramatic, and in some cases it is due to a total misunderstanding of what the person was trying to say.

Other Events

Political events and elections can also be major influencers. Someone who has a hawkish view of their currency, being elected to office could be a signal that the currency will appreciate.

Technical levels are also important with some currencies, especially with the round numbers that traders like to focus on. An example could be of a currency pair that is trading at 1.3995 and it has never been above 1.4000, then it begins moving even closer to 1.4000. This 1.4000 level could be seen as psychological that will be watched very closely, and if it is broken you could see what is called a breakout to the upside.

Using our example, if the currency pair is trading at 1.3995 and it goes above 1.4000, you might see that it shoots up to 1.4095 and then drops all the way back to 1.3995. Then we would say it was a false breakout, but there is the chance that it could be real and remain at the 1.4095 level.

Why do you want to trade FX?

You might be saying to yourself, all this is great info but why should I want to trade FX? There are many reasons.

Liquidity

Number one is liquidity, it is unmatched, there is nothing out there even close, as we mentioned at the beginning just a day of FX is two to three months of volume on the New York Stock Exchange. That is powerful.

24 Hour Trading

You have the 24 hour trading possibility, you can trade night or day. There is nothing else that offers this type of flexibility, and for the majority of traders who are business owners or have full time jobs, in some cases even university students, this is great.

Long or Short Option

FX gives the long or short option, this is very important. Traditionally most people are accustomed to being long, buying a particular share and hoping the share will increase in value. FX gives you the option of going short, it is a different way of looking at the market, but it can be lucrative. For the savvy traders it is a tool to use to take advantage of the market.

Correlation to other asset classes

Low correlation to other asset classes, this is important for those who are trying to have a diversified portfolio. When there is market turmoil, whether it is in commodities, or equities, Forex stands apart. Stocks can take a dive or commodity prices explode but Forex is Forex, it is moved by other forces. FX is not what you want to have as 80% of your portfolio, but having some exposure to FX is a prudent thing.

Basic FX Terms

I might not make you into a super trader overnight but having an understanding of these terms will make it easier to communicate in the FX community and also speak with your trading partners.

Your <u>base currency</u> is your market exposure, and the <u>variable currency</u> is used to calculate your profit and loss (P/ L). Taking a EURUSD example, the EUR is your base currency. Your exposure and your margin calculation will be done in Euro. The profit and loss will be done in USD.

Depending on the base currency of your account, your P/L will be calculated again, so for this example (EURUSD) and if you have Sterling (GBP) as your base currency then the profit and loss from US Dollars would then be converted to your base (GBP).

Basic terms continuing, we have EURUSD at 1.5800, what we are saying is 1 Euro is equivalent to 1.58 Dollars, or that the Euro is stronger than the US Dollar.

The Spread

This is a term that gets tossed around often amongst traders. The spread is the difference between the bid and the ask price. If on the <u>bid</u> the sell price is 1.5800 and the buy <u>ask</u> price is 1.5802, we have a 2 pips difference. We will say the spread is 2 pips.

Long, Short and Square

Long

You are buying,

Short

You are selling.

Examples

If you are long EURUSD or long Euro Dollar as we would say, then you are long Euro and you have sold or short USD. If you are short Euro Dollar, you are short Euros and long Dollars.

Square

You are closed. In clear terms to square a long 500,000 EURUSD position you need to short 500,000 EURUSD to remove your market exposure.

Trader jargon

This is a little extra that I have included for those of you who will be trading FX regularly.

First is **Cable (GBPUSD)**, a term you will hear repeatedly and it is Great British Pound against the US Dollar.

Swissie is the Swiss Franc (CHF)

Aussie is the Australian Dollar (AUD)

Kiwi is the New Zealand Dollar (NZD)

Loonie is the Canadian Dollar (CAD)

The Figure

Is OO at the end of a number, so sometimes while trading, you might speak to a dealer and he might say Euro Dollar is at "1.33 the figure" meaning 1.3300.

Stop Out

All your positions have been closed and it is something that you normally do not want to hear.

OCO

One cancels the other, is normally when you have a limit and stop order connected, if one gets filled the other is cancelled.

Filled

You now have the position. For example, you have a 3 way order that has the price level of where you want to enter the market, once that level is reached you are now filled.

A **quarter** is 250,000

A **half** is 500,000

One is one million

As stated, knowing these terms will make it easier to speak with your dealers or trading counterparts. For those thinking of getting into trading for a living then you definitely must know these terms.

FX Trade Calculations

Many people place FX trades, but most do not have an understanding of the things that are behind it. Before anyone gets into FX trading it is important that they are aware of the components in the margin, calculating the P/L, and the rollover principle. Let us review these areas.

Margin Requirements Awareness

At most FX houses traders are trading on margin and are not doing physical FX trading. The physical FX is where 1 dollar equals 1 dollar in value. With margin trading, you can open a 1 million EURUSD position, with a margin requirement of 1% which is 10,000 Euros. Another example, a 10,000 account balance with a 100,000 position would need 1,000 Euros to keep the position open.

Profit and Loss in Pips

Pips are the smallest price change that an exchange rate can make. We use EURUSD as an example, 1.5280 to 1.5281 is a one pip move. We have USDCAD 0.9955 it moves to 0.9956 also a one pip move.

Let us take an example of profit and loss in pips: Buy 100,000 EURUSD at 1.5100 take profit at 1.5160, 60 pips. You have a stop loss at 1.5070, 30 pips, this is from your entry position.

In pip terms we have here what is called a 2 to 1 ratio, when you go long EURUSD at 1.5100, take profit at 1.5160 and a stop loss at 1.5070.

Pip Value

There are several ways to calculate pip value. Since this is reality based guide we will use the simple way. Let us use the EURUSD example, which is quoted with 4 decimal places, ex. 1.5100, and a nominal value (the amount being traded) of 100,000.

First, count the amount of decimal places that you have and in this example it is 4. Starting from the right, remove 4 numbers from the nominal value (100,000) and you will get the value of each pip. Removing 4 zeros, show us that each pip is 10 Dollars. Remember as we covered earlier, the counter currency USD is used to calculate your profit and loss.

Taking it further, a 60 pip profit (60 x 10 USD) gives you 600 USD, or if you had a 30 pip loss (30 x 10) is 300 USD. When you are using ratio trading in your strategy, it must be that your chance of making a profit is greater than the chance of a loss.

Rollovers

This is something that has given FX traders headaches for many years, but it is not a complicated concept. A lot of people skip the rollover in training but we will address it here.

If you are long EURUSD, you are long Euro and short USD. You are holding Euros and you will earn interest on them. You are also borrowing or shorting USD, therefore you pay interest on what you borrow. The difference in interest is either positive or negative which is your swap.

On the reverse, if you are shorting EURUSD you are short Euros and long USD. You are borrowing the Euros in this case and you are now holding US Dollars. The interest difference is either positive or negative which is the swap.

EQUITY INVESTING

We will take a look at how the equity market is traded and review the things that I think are important when investing in equities.

Dividends

Dividends are a great place to begin. A dividend is income to a shareholder in addition to share value increase.

Companies offering dividends are normally blue chips. When you are looking at the components that one seeks in equity investing, this is one of them, remember this is equity investing not trading.

Companies offering dividends traditionally are well run if they were not, there would not be anything left over to pay dividends. This makes them a good alternative to bonds for the low risk investor.

Debt Levels

Debt is another of the factors to take into consideration when deciding to invest in a company. You want to look for what is called a low current asset to current liabilities ratio. Normally a ratio in the area of 1 to 3 is ok.

In some cases however, too much cash can be negative. It can be a sign of several things; they are not investing enough in the future, nothing is in the development pipeline. Excess cash could also mean they are not looking to make any strategic buys. Many say it is a sign of not enough proactive thinking on the part of the company's leadership.

Keep in mind that the ratio is relative to the sector that you are researching, for example, companies in the tech sector have debt ratios several times higher.

PE Ratio– Price to Earnings ratio

This is how much a company is worth on an exchange in relation to income from its product and services.

This is the most used method of valuing shares to see if they are priced right. You will hear the term repeatedly so it is important that you understand this concept. Using a simple example, if a firm has shares that are valued 50 million and the profits are 5 million, the P/E ratio is 10. As we discussed with assets to liability, the ratio is relative to the sector that you are researching.

Directors Trading

Directors are required to disclose when they trade shares in their companies. They are usually the most informed in the company so it might be a clue to future events, but keep an open mind.

Some people will say directors are selling because there is something negative going on in the company, or they are buying because there are aware of something positive. It is an indicator, but it is not a 100%, it could be something as mundane as they need the money. They might want to invest in other things or they are over exposed to that particular company's share and need to reduce. It also could be due to a divorce therefore it is not always a clear sign that something dramatic is happening.

Liquidity and Volume

Liquidity, as we touched on in the FX section is just as important in equity investing. I would say even more important with equity investing because, in FX you have the 24 hour opportunity to enter or exit trades. With physical shares, for the most part, exchanges are open between 9AM and 5PM depending on the country.

Liquidity and volume are important because they allow you to collect your profits with ease. It is great to look at paper profits but if you are unable to collect them it is not doing you all that much good. If you are facing a loss, then it can go from sad to a nightmarish scenario while looking at an increasing loss and being unable to exit it, therefore having liquidity is crucial.

Turn on your radar for OTCBB or pink sheets:

These are low liquidity shares that are traded on minor exchanges, be very wary of them. These shares are <u>not</u> normally subjected to the same auditing requirement as shares on major exchanges and mixed with low liquidity it is a recipe for sleepless nights.

Performance

How is your favorite shares' performance in relation to its peers? At the very least you want it to be equal, unless there is some special reason for the underperformance.

Performance over several time frames

If you are a long term investor, chasing the one week winner is usually not a sound investment strategy. Therefore select shares whose performance closely mirrors the time horizon of your investment strategy.

TESTED FOREX STRATEGIES | **25**

performance closely mirrors the time horizon of your investment strategy.

3 WAY ORDERS

The components of a 3 way order

Having satisfied your entry conditions, your initial order would be your <u>entry order</u>, sometimes called the primary order, it is the order used to enter the trade.

Next is your <u>limit order</u>, profit taking order, or as I say the fun order, this is where you are take your profits out of the market.

Finally we have the <u>stop loss order</u> which is used to limit your losses. A traders golden rule "no cash no trading", a stop loss is very important.

What are the advantages of 3 ways?

Remote Trading

3 way orders allow you to do remote trading. This is a great benefit for a lot of people, because most of us are working or running a business and do not have time to sit and watch trades minute by minute. With 3 way orders you can be active in the markets without being tied to your desk or news reports every second of the day.

Discipline

It instills discipline to your trading because the parameters are defined before you enter the trade and this is such an important point that we will revisit it. One thing is noted as the key difference between those who make a profit trading and those who are losing, is having the parameters set before trading.

Institutional traders, people whose profession is trading, they are using variations of these 3 ways orders. Where they will take profit and where they will cut the loss to preserve cash, is decided prior to entering the trade.

Minimizes the emotion of trading

When the parameters are predefined, it does not leave any room for you to interfere and start retooling everything in the middle of the trade. This is crucial.

Ratio trading

Ratio trading is your risk reward ratio and it is comprised of your entry level, stop loss and a take profit target. Ratio trading also refers to a win/loss ratio either 2 to 1, 3 to 1, etc.

We begin with a hypothetical trade. You have an entry price buying EURODOLLAR at 1.5550, you have a stop loss at 1.5525 which is 25 pips below, then you have a profit target at 1.5600, this is 50 pips. This combination gives you a ratio of 2 to 1.

Looking at a 3 way order with a 3 to 1 ratio, you buy EURUSD at 1.5550, stop loss 1.5525, 25 pips, and here we have a greater profit target 1.5625. The risk reward is 3 to 1.

Support and Resistance

With support and resistance levels we are getting to the basics of technical analysis. This is not meant to be a chapter on technical analysis, the intent is to give you the Practical Technical Analysis of what you need to know in order to place trades and hopefully make a profit.

Support Level

The support level is the price at which the instrument being traded has historically had difficulty falling below. Some people call it the floor. What is important to remember with the support level is that it changes along with your time frame. The support level that you see for an hour chart will be different from one that displays a day or a week. Therefore use a support and resistance level that matches your trading time frame.

Resistance Level

The resistance level is the price level where the currency or instrument that you are trading has historically had difficulty trading above.

The chart time frame should match your trading time horizon. A one hour resistance is totally different from a week's or a month's resistance. As with the support level the parameters must match up.

For those who would like to explore deeper into technical analysis, I have other resources that I can direct you to.

PUTTING IT ALL TOGETHER

n this section we will connect the different aspects of a trading system that traders ought to have.

Trading Platform

First, selecting your trading platform is obviously important because the platform is the vehicle that you use to conduct trading. The majority of us trade online and it is essential that you are using a platform that matches your style. It could be one that is either high tech or one that is more basic. You should also know the provider behind the platform. In a later section we will examine further the process of selecting a trading partner.

Goals

Without goals it is really difficult to begin trading. The analogy I heard and that I like to use in regards to goals is that without one it would be the equivalent of heading to an airline ticket counter and saying "give me a ticket!" And of course they would ask you "a ticket to where?"

Short term goals could be daily or weekly profit targets, they are individualized. Goals must match your style and the amount of risk capital available for trading.

Long term goals are often related to your investment strategy. They are also related to your short term goals because the long term goals should be based up on the short term profit targets. There must be a matchup, because if you have a weekly target of 100 dollars and a monthly target of a 1,000 then there is a discrepancy that needs to be addressed.

Finally, you must have a trading plan, because without one you are setting yourself up for potentially huge losses. With no plan there is no point in entering trading.

Mental Preparation

You do need to be psychologically ready to trade. If you are about to trade and are tense or nervous, then you need to take time off. Go meditate, get some exercise, do something else, but it is important that you do not trade until you are psychologically ready.

With trading you must have the mindset of not taking things personally. Remove emotions from trading, it is not an activity where it is you against the world. The goal is to make money.

Know your risk tolerance

How much are you willing to risk on each trade? It is important, remember golden rule number one, "no cash, no trading". It doesn't matter what anyone tells you, if there is no cash, there is no trading and this must be taken seriously.

This ties in with your risk tolerance, for example, having a cash balance of 10,000 USD and you want to risk 1%, the amount is 100 dollars. Meaning that of your risk capital, regardless of what you are trading, when you set your stop loss it should not exceed 100 USD.

Do your due diligence

A new day has begun and your computer is on, what happened overnight? What happened on the Nikkei? As a trader you must be updated on the correlation between markets.

For example, if you trade the Asian markets and live in Europe or the Caribbean, you should be aware of the news that came out overnight and more importantly how the markets reacted to it. Sometimes, what in theory should be good news the markets have a negative reaction.

Another example, traders have noticed that if the Nikkei opens negatively, many times the markets in Europe and the United States also opens negatively.

What is coming out today? If it is a report that can move the markets like Non-farm Payrolls, CPI, etc., then you need to look at your positions, particularly if you are trading FX which is very sensitive.

How to select your entry level

Knowing your entry points means you have a good reason for every trade that you execute. If you do not have a good reason, I suggest that you take the funds and turn them over to a charity. You must have a reason for selecting each trade.

When selecting your entry level, you need a good risk-reward ratio and this should match your risk tolerance.

Technical/fundamental analysis is also taken into consideration. The support and resistance levels, company earnings, government reports, are all essential before you execute any trade.

If you are trading FX you want to be aware of where the support and resistance lines are for the time frame that you are trading.

Know your exit levels

What is your profit target, is it a hundred dollars or a few? You need to be aware of this.

When you are setting stops to control losses, the first thing to do is to ensure that they fall within your parameters. If you are ratio trading, when setting the ratio, it should be at a level where you have a greater potential for profit than a loss.

Same as with your entry level, you should know the fundamental analysis, support and resistance levels, and another trader's golden rule "cut your losses and let profits run". Many traders say the profits take care of themselves but you must keep a close eye on the losses.

Keep a Journal

It might not be for everyone but it is something that I use to record my trading. It includes several things, where I entered the trade, my exit level, and why I thought the trade was a good idea when I entered it.

In review of your journal, if there are patterns, you will begin to detect them. You can either remove a pattern that is not working or expand on one that is. This helps you to fine tune your trades.

Review Your Results

Review your profit or loss for the day. It is important because while trading can be fun, it is a business and the point is to make a profit. In the review of your P/L and it is not what you had intended, your duty is to find out why.

You need to know what was behind your results. Maybe it was pure luck, and if that was the case, great, but luck is normally not a sustainable strategy for trading. I would suggest, as I do in my trading, review your journal. Were the trades timed correctly with a report that came out? Or was it the size of the positions? These factors can influence the results.

Next step, are you aware of tomorrow's news releases? As you scan the reports, you can be proactive about future trades. Depending on the data that is being released you might want to get in the market early.

TRADING TACTICS

Here we will examine the major reasons why traders lose money and most important we will explore the solutions.

Unrealistic Expectations

It is important when getting into trading, as with many things, one must have a realistic idea of what you are dealing with. Unrealistic expectations can take the form of someone starting with what is sometimes called a mini-trader account of 1,000 or maybe 2,000 USD and expecting overnight riches.

I have even seen where you can even begin with 100 or 200 dollars which is fine. There is nothing wrong with the amount, but those same traders at 100 or 200 dollars are expecting to have 1,000 or 2,000 dollars in their accounts within a few weeks or even in a couple days. There are firms out there who have actually mentioned or even promised them that they can do this. While I am not saying it is impossible, I am saying it is unrealistic. It is essential that you do have a sense of reality to your trading.

No Plan

No plan as we have discussed, would be similar to arriving at an airline counter and saying "give me a ticket", which does not make much sense. With planning, your trading needs to have an alignment of timeframe and the results that you are expecting to receive.

If you like FX then it is a good idea to stick with FX and build a base from there and later explore other instruments. Maybe even begin trading FX futures because once you have a good understanding of FX then you can start looking into offshoots of it, for example in the futures markets.

If you are familiar with trading equities then you might want to explore CFDs (Contracts For Difference) which are equity derivatives. They are traded by active traders. Again it is all working with the plan that you must have to begin.

Too Much Risk

It could be the person with 100 dollars in their account or even 100,000. It is not the amount that is critical, but the amount you are risking in relation to the funds available.

A simple example, if you have 10,000 USD in your account and are trading a 100,000 EURUSD position, each pip is 10 dollars. This is not that much, which is fine depending on your risk profile. If you then switch to trading a 1,000,000 position each pip is now worth 100 dollars. If you have 10,000 USD in your account and you are long, a 10 pip move lower leaves you automatically with a loss of 1,000 dollars.

Confusing Trading With Investing

In my years as a banker, I have had countless clients who I had to again and again point out that they should not confuse the two. Trading is about making money, it is income generating activity. You are moving in and out of trades, unlike investing which is more long term. It could be that some of your investment goals are derived from your trading but do not confuse them.

The instruments that you are trading, for example FX which is active, you are not investing you are trading, and hopefully earning income. Another example could be CFDs.

It might seem basic to some, but speaking from experience of advising clients globally there are still many out there that get trading and investment confused.

Solutions

It's ok to talk about problems and challenges, but obviously we need to have some solutions.

Low Leverage

We discussed the problems with too much risks, the solution is using low leverage. You plan to open a 100,000 dollar position on EURUSD where each pip is worth 10 dollars, if you are not 100% sure of this trade you might want to begin with 50,000. You keep the leverage low because it gives you time to think, to react more effectively, and you are not as sensitive to changes in the market.

Scaling In Scaling Out

Scaling in scaling out is one of my favorites. I use it with investing and also with my trading. Scaling in scaling out, the theory behind it is that you allow the market to tell you which way to go, it is that simple.

An example, I plan to buy 1,000 shares of GCMS after having done my technical and fundamental analysis. How to begin? I would start with a 200 or 250 shares position and allow the market to confirm if I am on the right path. If I bought GCMS shares at 100 dollars and they suddenly jump to 125 per share, great, the marketing is confirming that I made the correct decision. In this example if I began with 200 shares, I would then add another 200 or 250 and repeat the process until I reach my goal of a 1,000 shares.

There are some who might say I missed out a little on the move from 100 to 125 and I did somewhat, but I am also more secure in my decision by being patient. On the reverse, getting back to scaling out, let us say if the market had moved against me, instead of having 1,000 shares at risk initially, it would have been only 200. Obviously there is a trade off, but from experience, it is to the advantage of those who are scaling in scaling out.

Another example, let us say you bought 200 shares at 100 dollars each and the price suddenly drops to 90. What I would suggest, instead of selling everything immediately, that you consider selling only 50 or 75 because the drop could be due to an overreaction in the market. There are several things that could be at play, for example a false rumor, again you are allowing the market to guide you along the correct path. Of course if the price continues to fall then you sell more. Another way to look at it, using the analogy of driving on the highway, if you have a long straightaway you speed up and if you have a lot of curves you slow down, it seems to work.

Trade Liquid Markets

To trade liquid markets is something I can't overemphasize. There are people in the equity market that trade Over the Counter Bulletin Board (OTCBB) or other thinly traded shares and in FX it is exotic currencies (often low liquidity) which is fine, as long as you are aware of the risk.

Liquidity is critical especially as a trader, an investor is not as time sensitive, but if you are trading where you do need to make sudden moves you want to be in a liquid market.

Liquid, to be very clear, is the ability to come in and out of the trade with ease. Being in a trade and having paper profits is wonderful, but when it is time to convert the paper profits and if you are unable to do so, then it is a bad joke as you can only watch them, not very nice. On the other side if you are in a loss and are unable to exit that position, it turns into a nightmare. I don't care who is giving tips, or whatever blog you are reading, you must trade liquid markets, there is no other way.

News Trading

This is for the news traders out there and if you are thinking of trading over numbers (when market data is being released) think again.

There are different systems that these traders use to trade over numbers in an attempt to be smarter than the banks, all I can say is that it is a tactic I would not suggest. First of all, the banks are not stupid they know who their clients are and they have departments set up to monitor this type of activity to ensure that they are not being cheated.

If you want to trade over numbers, be aware that the price where your order might get filled or executed could be very different from what you had in mind. For those who trade with providers who guarantee pricing, I would wager that 9.99 out of 10 have a clause in the fine print that states the guarantee is only valid under normal market conditions. Meaning that over numbers the price that you see might not be what you will get.

Selecting Currency Pairs

In FX select a few pairs and get to know them like a close friend. A lot of people begin FX by trading the "majors", EURUSD, GBPUSD, USDCAD, USDJPY, or AUDUSD for example. Of the majors, get to know a few of them well whether it is EURSEK/Euro Swedish, for those in the Scandinavian market or EURJPY for those in the rest of Europe.

Personally, I trade only three or four for the most part. After a while once you begin trading these currency pairs they will become familiar and you will get a deeper sense of how they move.

Other Tactics

In CFDs or shares, company upgrades, profit warnings are good opportunities meaning that prices tend to go in the direction of the announcement. So if they announce an upgrade chances are prices will head up. And the other side, at least statistically, when companies announce profit warnings, prices tend to go down. However, many times by the end of the quarter those same companies beat the lower estimates that they had announced which leads to a share increase. So for the daring, you can buy after the initial price drop from the announcement. This could be your lottery ticket trade.

Placing orders Strategically

You want to be first in line when getting your orders filled, and placing limits orders before the resistance is effective because the resistance levels are known to everyone already. You want to get filled right before it hits resistance if you are a technical trader and at support you either want to be a little above it or a little beneath the support level if long, just to make sure it wasn't a false breakout to the downside.

Use the Principles of Delta

Delta trading or the principles of delta trading have been around for many years. It began with a select group of people who were called the Delta Society. They paid a lot of money to join and learn the principles, which had been covered in mystery and mystique.

The main principles are that when someone is trading (not investing), that you see the market almost through the eyes of a child. Shares that are going up will continue to go up, therefore you buy them, and those that are going down will continue to do so. Nothing is overbought or oversold you simply go along with the market.

There are some tools that are needed to execute the strategy. First, you need to trade active stocks those that are trading sideways are not applicable to the strategy. You should also use a stock filter which is a great tool, and most are free.

The filters help you to efficiently locate shares that are going up and the ones that are going down. What I have seen that works best when using filters is to find the winners across the different time frames.

An example would be to first filter for the three month winners. Then filter deeper to find the one month winners, and finally look at the one week winners. This filtering process allows you to see which shares are consistently coming up winners across the time frames. These are shares that people want. Armed with this data you have a better basis for selecting shares to buy for your trading portfolio.

This is a trading technique not investing, because the one week or one month winners might not be the stocks that you want for your long term investment portfolio. Just by using the principles of filtering out the 3, 1 month, or 1 week winners you are ahead of many. Depending on the aggressiveness of your trading style is that you can alter the time frames to your taste. It is a technique I have used with strong results.

To conclude, the most successful traders use a system. They have a set entry, exit, position size, and they are going to scale in/out. As we covered at the beginning you must have a plan, it is what separates the professionals from gamblers.

SELECTING A TRADING PARTNER

We will review the important aspects of selecting a trading partner.

What is Important?

Liquidity

Liquidity at all times, especially in periods of volatility as we discussed in previous sections, it is so important that we mention it again. Your trading partner must be able to provide you with it.

It is important for the instruments that you are trading, whether it is FX or shares. FX crosses are liquid but you also need to be with a partner that has access to this liquidity or else you could be in the bad joke situation where you have a profit but are unable to collect.

Fast Execution

Fast execution, so that when you click, you get the indicated price. Liquidity is a key factor in execution speed.

Trustworthy

As with any type of relationship, you want to be with a trading partner that has a good reputation and is known for being trustworthy and has a solid financial base. You do not want to trade with someone that is at risk of collapsing. Getting a recommendation from a trusted friend is encouraged.

Reliable platform

Your platform needs to be reliable. It is not optimal to have a platform that is often down when you are ready to trade or has lots of technical issues.

When trading during normal market conditions and if you are frequently getting re-quoted prices, that is a red flag.

Access to news and market data

Your platform or trading partner should have access to news or to what is sometimes called streaming news from the different news agencies for ex Reuters, Bloomberg. You also want to get access to their market making desk. If they do not have one, they should be able to provide you with market flow data, for example if traders are currently long EURUSD or there seems to be a movement to USDJPY. This is important, in particular when trading Forex.

Best in class strategy team

No strategy team is perfect, but you do want one that is reliable and that you trust is giving you unbiased market analysis. As with the other topics you want to speak with friends to get their opinions on the recommendations from the strategy teams they deal with.

Reliable Charting System

We have a saying that charts are for "indicative purposes only", they are not the market, yet you want charts that give a good idea of where the market is. Another factor, depending on the charting system, the chart will only reflect the bid (sell price).

In my years of working at a trading desk, I have had numerous discussions with clients after a "bad fill" (trading jargon, for your trade was executed at a price worse than what you expected). In these disputes clients would look at the chart and say "but the chart says this, and this is what I want to get", very important point, the chart is indicative the chart is not the market.

Any broker that you deal with, you want them to trade at where the market is and not the chart. The best words of advice when dealing with a professional dealer or institutional broker over a trade dispute, is that you discuss the market price and stay away from what the chart says. If they are professionals the first thing they will mention to you is where the market was and not where the chart was, because people trade the markets not charts.

How do you find the good guys?

Speak to friends who are trading and of course you may contact me.

Forex News Trading Code

1-Orders only - only in the market when there is noticeable move. This allows me to avoid non-trending markets(money loser, only the broker makes money here)

2-Having buy or sell stop entry orders 10-20 pips above where we are trading means I don't enter unless there is a real move in the market(avoid false breakouts and market fakes this way). Yes, I'm aware I wil miss some of the initial market move but this is offset by getting NOT suckered by false breakouts.

3- Don't trade as often as others but when I do there is movement. Losses are set by stop loss(before the trade)

4-Most important stop loss set at max 12-15 pips. See point below.

Trading is a **business = money management** not a silly game about if you are "right or wrong" only make or lose money.

TECH ANALYSIS
TRADE GUIDE

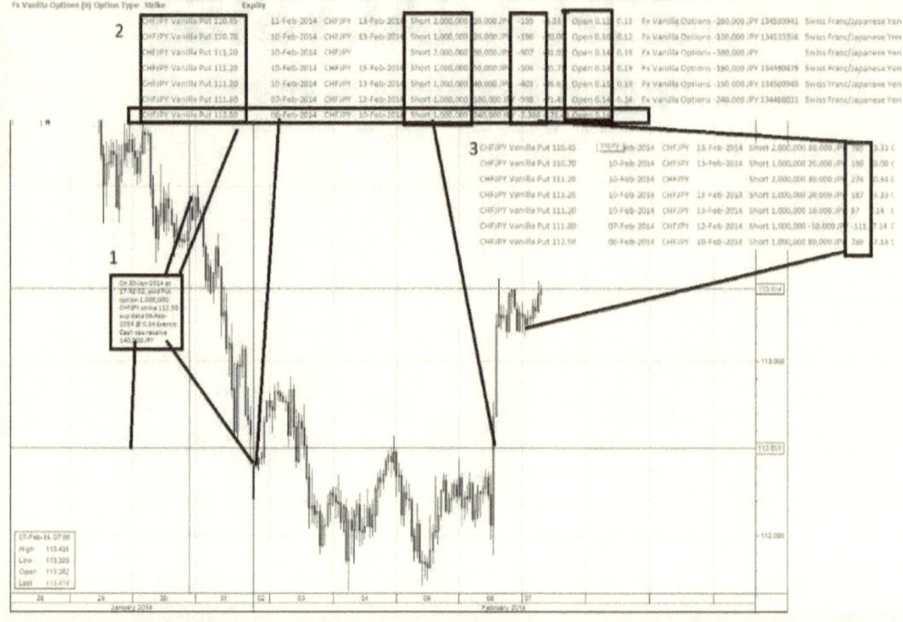

Chart Time Frame

Time frame, the most critical factor of a trading decision. The decision to buy or sell <u>always</u> begins with the time frame. A signal to buy or sell for a day trader is different from a swing trader and in a most cases extremely different from a long term trader/investor. The examples we will use are based on short term/day trading time frames.

Day trading – Closing positions within 24 hours

Swing trading – Holding trades open from a few hours to maximum a few days

For short term traders a chart setting of 1 hour is good for getting a market overview, and then making the decision to trade off the 30 or

15 minutes chart. The shorter your trading time horizon the shorter you chart time frame.

To use the settings above it's recommended that you create charts of different time frames and leave them open on your trading platform. This will make it more efficient to trade.

Time frame & your location in the buy – sell channel

Once the time frame has been set, you need to locate out where you are in the trade channel (the trade channel is the area between the high and low bands of the Bollinger Bands). If you are near the top of the channel that indicates that you are close to a potential reversal level (where the market turns/reverses)...ex if heading up, it suddenly heads down. If at the bottom and the market heads up it's also a reversal level.

What to do at reversal levels

This is where trading gets a bit tricky. Just because we are at or near a reversal level it's no guarantee that it will reverse. We could also get a breakout (the market going above/below known resistance or support levels). One tip in figuring out what to do next, is to simply review the chart for past market movements(did it go up or down)at the price level you are looking to see what happened in the market the last time. This is important because the central "person" here is the market <u>not</u> you).

For example, if the market headed down then there is a good chance that it will do that again. However this is NOT a guarantee, and you also need to be aware of fundamental data(news report, economic data) as this could throw everything off from the result of the last time.

If you don't have a position open already, and the market is at a potential reversal level, one way to trade it is setting a buy order above the reversal level. Therefore if the market does get the breakout then you are in. The buy order is also part of your risk management because there is only money on the table if it gets executed and becomes a trade.

After figuring out where you are in the buy/sell channel you now want to pay attention to the RSI and what it is telling you. You need to have a match between that and your trade execution. So if the RSI is at overbought levels and you are near reversal levels on the Bollinger bands then it is a sign of a good potential sell opportunity.

Ideal buy signals

Ideally on a buy signal you want your RSI to be heading up from at or near the 30-40 levels giving good room/opportunity to head up. At the same time you also want the market to be located/trading near the bottom of the channel in the Bollinger Bands.

Finally, if using candle stick charts you will want them to be green (prices closing up). As you can see we need to see the same data(up) from our tools. Looking at red candle sticks(prices closing lower) and overbought (excessive buying) RSI levels is a mixed signal. This tell you to "stand aside"... do not trade until things are clearer.

Ideal sell signals

An ideal sell signal is simply the opposite of the above. In other words, your RSI will be heading <u>down</u> from 70-80 levels. At the same time you also want the market to be located/trading near the top of the channel in the Bollinger Bands. Finally, if using candle stick charts you will want them to be red (prices closing down).

Wrapping up

Ideally you want to execute a trade from when things are as close to ideal as possible. When faced with grey areas/undecided we suggest that you use buy or sell orders. Orders are NOT trades so no money is at risk until they are executed. These orders will be placed near the ideal levels that you are seeking to trade from.

As we have stressed several times, ideal trade scenario or not, you always place a stop order. Unfortunately, even the world's best research is no guarantee of a profitable trade.

Settings for the technical analysis tools

RSI

One RSI, the default of 14 is fine for most FX, CFD, equity trading. However with shorter term trading day trading or swing trading then

14 is not optimal. We suggest 7 for swing trading and down to 4 for day trading.

Bollinger Bands

The default settings of seems to work best for most traders and we suggest that you keep this setting.

Moving Averages

We use 50, 100, 200. The 50 is the alert signal, 100 short term and 200 is the long term.

GCMS TRADING DIPLOMA

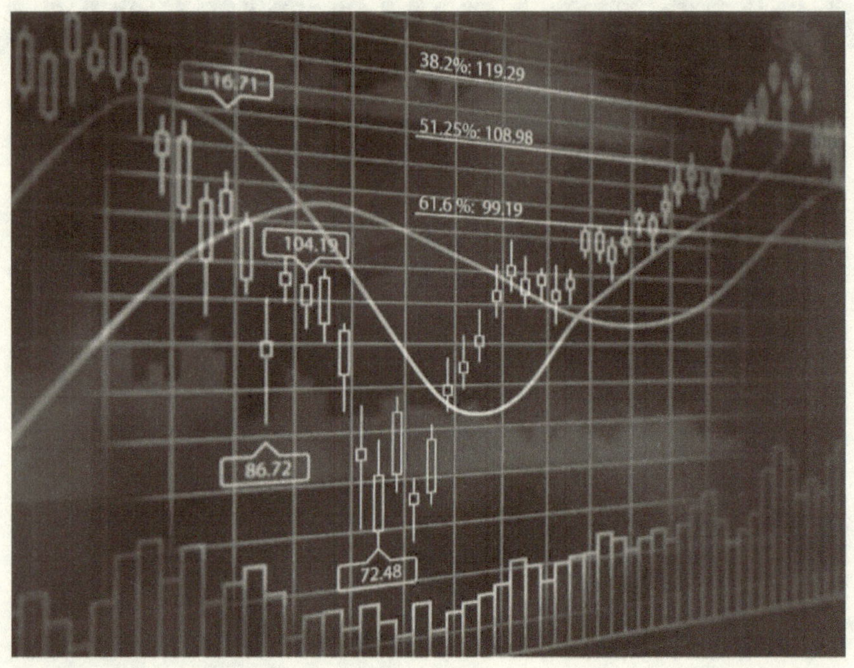

Basics of a Trading System

-Time Frame

-Tool that identify a trend

-Tools that help confirm/filter the trend

-Establish your risk tolerance (position sizing)

-Select entry-exit levels

-Follow your rules

Note:

Doing your homework does <u>not</u> guarantee your trade will be profitable, but it does increase your odds.

If technical or fundamental data is unclear or "messy" you do have the right not to trade.

PROFILE OF THE AUTHOR

Wayne Walker is the Director of a global capital markets education and consulting firm (gcmsonline.info). He has several years experience in leading and coaching teams of Investment Advisors and has managed top performing teams in the Private Client Group based on Bench Mark Earnings (BME). Mr. Walker has trained traders of the Citi-FX Pro program in London. He also developed the 'Trading Rights' program at Saxo Bank by which Investment Advisors were required to complete before being allowed to trade. He is a certified trader by Markets in Financial Instrument Directive (MiFID) EU and is qualified to advise "A" clients.

Mr. Walker is a frequently invited guest capital markets commentator on several live international TV & radio programs.

Mr. Walker holds several certifications and has worked in the following positions:

- Director-Founder, (GCMS) Global Capital Market Solutions, Denmark

- Manager, Sales Trading, North America & Middle East, Saxo Bank, Denmark

- B.sc State University of New York, College at Buffalo, USA

- NASD Series 3 – License to trade & advise on futures contracts in the US Market

- ACI(Financial Markets) Dealing Certificate – Passed with Distinction (highest level), France

- Trained in Bloomberg & UBS Bank's FX Options quoting software

www.ingramcontent.com/pod-product-compliance
Lightning Source LLC
Chambersburg PA
CBHW020935160726

47993CB00007B/2797